Fairy Gardening 101

Miniature equipment for a fairy gardener,
photo courtesy of Rose Mannering

Fairy Gardening 101

How to Design, Plant, Grow, and Create Over 25 Miniature Gardens

Fiona McDonald

Skyhorse Publishing

Skyhorse Publishing books may be purchased in bulk at special discounts for sales promotion, corporate gifts, fund-raising, or educational purposes. Special editions can also be created to specifications. For details, contact the Special Sales Department, Skyhorse Publishing, 307 West 36th Street, 11th Floor, New York, NY 10018 or info@skyhorsepublishing.com.

Skyhorse® and Skyhorse Publishing® are registered trademarks of Skyhorse Publishing, Inc.®, a Delaware corporation.

Visit our website at www.skyhorsepublishing.com.

10 9 8 7 6 5 4 3 2 1

Library of Congress Cataloging-in-Publication Data

McDonald, Fiona.

  Fairy gardening 101 : how to design, plant, grow, and create over 25 miniature gardens / Fiona McDonald.

     pages cm

  Other title: How to design, plant, grow, and create over 25 miniature gardens

  ISBN 978-1-62914-179-4 (pbk. : alk. paper)   1. Gardens, Miniature.   2. Miniature plants.   I. Title. II. Title: How to design, plant, grow, and create over 25 miniature gardens.

  SB433.5.M33 2014

  635—dc23

                                2014007189

Cover design by Eve Siegel
Cover photos by Fiona McDonald

ISBN: 978-1-62914-179-4
Ebook ISBN: 978-1-62914-282-1

Printed in China

To my granddaughters, Isabelle and Charlotte,
who often look for fairies in the garden.

CONTENTS

Introduction

Photo courtesy of Patti at Wholesale Fairy
Gardens

Thorn, Ash and Oak are their favorite trees
So perhaps you could circle the boughs with these:
Some Foxgloves for thimbles, some Thyme for a treat
Bluebells for their magic and logs for a seat!
Plant Primrose and eat them if you dare by the day
and it is said by the evening you'll glance a few Fey!

Believe in the fairies who make dreams come true.
Believe in the magic from the fairies above,
They dance in the flowers and sing songs of love.
And if you believe and always stay true,
The fairies will be there to watch over you.

—John Atkinson Grimshaw

Who hasn't once gone looking for fairies at the edge of the garden? My cousin and I were always peering into roses, under daisies, and in the overgrown honeysuckle hoping to catch the briefest glimpse of a tiny winged being. A flicker of iridescent blue, a flash of soft pink, and a giggle that was gone before it had begun; these were surely signs of fairies inhabiting our garden oasis.

If you believe in these tiny nature spirits and would really like to make their acquaintance, then there are ways of enticing them into your garden. Of course, if you have a large, overgrown, and private yard, you are halfway there. Fairies are timid of us big folk and need places to hide in case of danger.

Fairies adore flowers, so plants with lots of color and pretty aroma are very attractive to them. A variety of sizes is a good idea as well. Tiny flowers can be used by fairy maidens as headdresses and garlands; larger flowers can become luxurious beds on which fairies can rest after a hard day's work.

Trees, too, are a great addition if your garden is big enough. Fairies have natural affinities with certain trees: oak, elm, ash, blackthorn, hazel, and alder are preferred, as are thorn bushes. Some of these have their own special spirits. Willow trees, for example, contain spirits that are a lot like cranky old men and have been known to pull up their roots during the night and to move around. Rowan, on the other hand, was often used to ward off evil spirits, including members of the fairy folk.

A Brief History of Fairies

By the craggy hill-side,
Through the mosses bare,
They have planted thorn-trees
For pleasure here and there.
Is any man so daring
As dig them up in spite,
He shall find their sharpest thorns
In his bed at night
—William Allingham

Fairy beings belong to all cultures and all times but the word *fairy* itself has an interesting origin and was not in use before the Middle Ages. It evolved out of the Italian word *fatae*, which was the name given to fairy ladies who were guests at christenings and who were called upon to bless the child (and we all know that it is a bad move to forget to invite any of these or your child might be given a century-long nap). It was a name that came from the pre-Christian belief in the Fates, who were integrated into Roman mythology from Ancient Greece.

The French took the word *fatae* from their Italian neighbors and made it *faie* and added *erie*, but even though the result sounded like the word we know today its meaning was one of being enchanted. Over time, faerie changed to become a noun referring to a supernatural race of creatures from the Celtic fairy realm. This included the Seelie Court (fair and good) and the Unseelie Court (dark and wicked), trooping fairies (sometimes human sized who like to parade on their beautiful horses in sparkling armor), pixies, elves, leprechauns (typically Irish), brownies, boggles, boggarts, banshees, and tiny winged humans with mischievous magic powers.

It is this last group—the tiny winged humans—that most of us now think of when we say "fairy," and it is this group that *Fairy Gardening 101* is aiming to attract into your own special garden. Now, although this is what we will attempt to do I'm afraid I cannot accept any responsibility if you also attract hobgoblins, gnomes, or cobblynau into it, too. It is a fact that magic is beautiful, but it is not without risk (but I think the possibility of having a garden full of fairies is worth it).

Chapter 1

Things You Might Need to Create Your Fairy Garden

You really do not need any expensive or exotic equipment in order to make a fairy garden. There is, however, one absolutely essential ingredient and that is imagination. Without it, I am afraid that all the best efforts of the best gardeners in the world will not succeed in bringing fairies into your garden.

It is possible to go into your own backyard or into the woods, say, when you are on a picnic, and fashion a garden out of the things around you—and the result can be most satisfying. Having said that, there are a few things that make fairy gardening of any sort a little easier and more comfortable.

I like to dig earth and deal out potting soil with a trowel. We have several ancient examples kicking around the home and these weathered work tools are just the thing for digging in the soil, helping remove weeds, and back-filling potting soil.

An old butter knife is also a useful tool for making small holes in the dirt for small plants. My mother always had one sitting next to her trowel beside the back door and I recommend you keep one near your fairy garden as you plant it.

You will also need some sort of potting soil. (I do know one person who used soil straight from the garden mixed with horse manure for their fairy garden but the result was rather lumpy.) Potting soil is cheap and readily available at the most garden centers and even a few supermarkets. It gives a nice even finish to the top of the garden bed as well.

A watering can is a good idea, too, and I recommend having two of different sizes—one tiny and one medium. But even a bucket and plastic container, like a margarine container, work just as well.

Gardening gloves are also a helpful tool when working on your garden. There are usually warnings about handling potting soil with bare hands, so gloves come in handy when using any sort of packaged soil. Furthermore, gloves are essential for working with cacti—believe me—and the thicker the glove, the better (I used leather gardening gloves for working with cacti and still got prickles in me). Just watch how you handle small or delicate plants with gloves on as it does make it difficult to use your fingers dexterously.

Of course, you will also need plants for your fairy garden. You will either want live plants or you may want artificial ones, too. You can buy plants especially for your fairy garden at certain garden centers. Some basic foundational plants for your fairy garden include: pansies, polyanthus, snapdragons, violas and violets, petunias, and azaleas. Most importantly, though, choose whatever is in season, whatever is suitable for the climate you live in, and whatever will flourish in the spot where you are going to place your fairy garden. For instance, if you live in a part of the country that gets heavy frosts, don't put delicate plants into your fairy garden unless they are going to be extremely well protected from the elements. Likewise, don't put sun loving plants in deep shade, nor those that love moist, cool conditions in the blazing sun. Creating a flourishing, long-lasting fairy garden is about using common sense and reading the growing and watering instructions that come with the plant.

Also be aware of the estimated size of your fully grown plants. At first, a particular plant might look sweet and charming at the seedling stage, but it then may grow too big for the pot you've chosen or die because of lack of room. Some plants tolerate being stunted in their growth—a sort of natural bonsai—by being kept in a small pot and trimmed. Again, read the instructions for whichever plants you are thinking of using or do a little online research if you are not sure what plants will work best for your fairy garden.

There are other ways of acquiring plants rather than buying them at the nursery or garden center. You can plant seeds and grow foliage from there, take cuttings, swap some with your neighbor, or even sneak a piece of plant off as you walk past one (only don't destroy the plant in the process—and don't take anyone's plants from their yard without asking first). Remember that different plants will propagate using different processes. Again, if you are not sure about a certain plant's growing and watering habits, do some research first. The internet is really a one-stop shop for information on most plants or you can go about it the old-fashioned way by checking a book out of the library.

Here's a very important tip: What really makes a fairy garden attractive to fairies is the accessories you choose to include in your fairy garden. A pot full of small plants will probably only look like a pot full of small plants to a fairy. It will be pretty, certainly, but there will be nothing to designate it as being a true fairy garden.

Hence, this is where accessories play a vital role in attracting fairies to your special garden. This is also what I consider the most enjoyable part of creating a fairy garden. In chapter 15, I will provide step-by-step instructions on how to make some of your own fairy garden furniture as well as give tips on finding store-bought fairy accessories. Another really fun way to find fairy garden treasures is to visit a thrift store or second-hand shop and see what grabs your fancy—as well as your imagination.

In the past, I have bought little ceramic pots and dishes at the second-hand shops in order to create my fairy gardens. These make great ponds or garden pots for your fairy gardens. Ceramic coasters can also make nice patios. Shell ornaments, miniature vases, resin ornaments, plastic flowers, little animal figurines, tiny baskets—all of these can be useful and decorative

in your fairy garden. All you must really do is simply think of what a fairy might use a particular item for. For example, an old tea cup is far too big for a fairy to drink tea out of, but it could make a lovely bowl for a fountain or, lined with some fine straw, it could become a great nest-type bed for a sleepy fairy. Keep Popsicle sticks, matchsticks, champagne wires and corks, and even the lids of drink bottles for use in your fairy garden (bottle lids actually make good plant sized pots for fairies).

In my time creating fairy gardens, I've also discovered an excellent source of fairy garden furniture in the aquarium section of certain pet stores. Old bridges, imitation logs, and the like make rather intriguing accessories for a miniature garden. Also, while in the supermarket or craft store, head down the toy aisle and look out for dolls' house furniture, benches, and such. Even if you find something that isn't the right color fit for your fairy garden, do not worry! You can always paint it with any acrylic paint of your choosing to match your fairy décor.

It would be easy to have a large discussion about things such as scale and ratios in designing fairy gardens, and while working in such a way is admirable and has its place, it isn't always necessary in order to make a beautiful garden suitable for fairies. One problem of working to scale is that fairies themselves come in various shapes and sizes. Just take the trooping fairies who are reportedly often as large as humans, so your standard fairy garden would be much too tiny for them. When setting out to create a miniature garden, I go by the ancient rule of thumb: if it looks good then do it. Does it really matter if the chair is a little too big or a plant a little too small? The best thing to do, though, is to try as best you can to keep objects in proportion with each other unless you want the difference to be a focal point.

Another point worth mentioning when you are preparing to create a fairy garden is that you don't need to have any formal plan when gardening (whether for fairies

or otherwise). Personally, I like to let ideas grow organically and for there to be a slight sense of disorder in my garden (although not actually chaos). This doesn't mean that you can't draw up plans or themes before making gardens—and certainly if you want a formal garden you will probably need measurements and a well thought-out idea of how you want the finished product to turn out.

One last—but very important—item you may want to include in your magic garden is a fairy figurine. While I am sure real fairies will want to visit your beautiful creation, they will probably not do so while being watched. So to enjoy the total effect of your miniature creation, you should feel free to put some fairy figures into the tableaux. Your fairy will certainly not scare off any real fairies from visiting either. Pretty resin fairies are readily available from fairy wholesalers, garden centers, and any of the other stores mentioned previously. The faces and attire of these fairies can be repainted if you have a fine brush and a steady hand to create a truly unique fairy just for your special garden. Small plastic dolls are also options for your garden, especially if you dress them in some tulle, let their hair out, and add artificial butterfly wings to the back of their clothes.

You can even make your own fairies from scratch! I have included instructions to create a tiny knitted fairy, a slightly bigger cloth fairy, as well as a bead head and pipe cleaner fairy so you can have a holistic handmade approach to your garden if you like.

Last but most certainly not the least is your imagination and the willingness to experiment. And above all: enjoy yourself as you set out to create your own magical miniature garden.

Fairy Garden Maintenance

The truth is that even fairy gardens need upkeep—and don't think you can rely on the fairies themselves to do any weeding! While a little bit of wildness in your garden can be attractive, you certainly don't want all of your hard work to be taken over by weeds or to die from lack of water or exposure to cold. Fairy gardens are smaller than your typical garden, so they need just a little daily or weekly maintenance (depending on what plants you've chosen for your particular garden) and if you expect frost, be sure to cover your garden or move it into a more temperature-controlled environment. Above all, just give your little garden love and it will be sure to last a long time and invite fairies for years to come.

Chapter 2

Basic Fairy Gardens

The best way to learn about fairy gardening is to roll up your shirt sleeves and make your own. Keep your first garden simple, as you can always add to it later as you gain more confidence and experience.

It is important to remember that there is a difference between a simple potted garden and a fairy garden. A potted garden consists of just plants while a fairy garden requires the gardener to imagine (and plan for) building an environment for tiny people who will want to do some of the things humans do in the garden: sit, swing, lie in a hammock, sip cool drinks, and enjoy the ever changing light playing through leaves and flowers.

Child's Play

The first garden we are going to make is super easy. It only requires a pot, potting soil, a small selection of plants, tiny cork tiles, pebbles, shells, a wire chair, and a fairy of your choosing.

You can imagine how excited my granddaughter Isabelle (Izzy) was when she learned that her granny was writing a book all about making fairy gardens! Of course, we had to begin with a garden that was all her own and one that is easy for any child to make. Just follow these simple steps and you'll be well on your way to a fabulous and enchanted fairy garden!

- Because we were in such a rush to start Izzy's garden we did not wait to go and buy a special pot. Instead, we used one that was lurking behind a pile of boxes in the shed. Izzy had a choice of rectangular or round and she chose rectangular.

After brushing away the dust and cobwebs (which was Granny's job, of course) we filled the pot with potting soil. We used a low-priced brand from the garden center.

2. We did, however, have to go to the store soon after getting the pot ready in order to buy some plants. At the nursery, we chose some polyanthus because they had just come into season in the early spring. Polyanthus are very colorful and hardy and are also inexpensive, so perfect plants to use on a budget. There were some miniature box plants on sale, too, and we chose one of those as well as some tiny containers with a special grass in them. Of course we bought more than we needed for one small garden and Izzy had some tough decisions to make.

3. Before planting, the potting soil needs a drop of water so that the newly uprooted plants won't get too big a shock when inserted in new dirt.

4. Now it is time to get down to business. Children will probably need help digging holes and inserting plants into them, depending on their age and experience. Be sure to give the plants plenty of room and back fill the holes carefully, patting the earth down to make it firm.

5. Isabelle planted three plants in a row at the back of her pot and a second tuft of grass in front of the first. This is so she can make a real feature of the path she wants to put along the front of the garden.

6. Now comes the really exciting part that turns a pot of plants into a magical fairy garden. Isabelle started to place her cork circles on the soil to create a path. She pushed the little tiles down into the soil as best she could to make them look as though they were paving stones. Then Isabelle decided to see how a border of little shells would look beside the cork path.

7. Finally, there were only two morc things needed to complete the garden: a fairy chair (the instructions for making this and other pieces of garden furniture are given in chapter 15) and the fairy herself. (Isabelle later removed the fairy (a resin replica) so that real fairies wouldn't be afraid to come and use the garden.)

8. And voila! A beautiful—and simple—fairy garden that is perfect for any beginner—child or adult!

Granny's Garden

Isabelle had so much fun making her little fairy garden that I couldn't resist making a simple one, too. I had this lovely little pot sitting around for years just collecting dust. It had once contained a bonsai but it had died not long after being purchased. The container, however, is a delightful handmade ceramic with one side designed to hold water and a bridge built into the hole. Needless to say, it was the perfect pot for attracting fairies!

To create a similar garden, find your favorite pot and follow these simple steps.

1. Fill the larger part of the pot with potting soil. Try not to get any in the part that will have water in it as it is really hard to get it out when the other side has been planted and it will make the water dirty.

2. The plants in this pot need to be small and to stay relatively small so choose varieties that will not need to be transplanted too soon. For my garden I chose a clump of ornamental grass and placed it next to the minature ivy. I'm not certain how big the grass will grow so I may have to pull it out if it gets too large, but for now, it will suffice.

3. There is not a lot of room in this tiny garden so I decided not to add any more plants in. When you don't have a lot of room for plants, think about adding some pebbles instead. This will make a nice area for fairies to sunbathe next to their pool and the pebbles also add a bit of color to the garden, which can be quite dark due to the plants chosen.

4. Finishing touches I used were a champagne wire chair (instructions are given in chapter 15) and some more shells in the bottom of the pond. In addition to giving a nice finish to the pond, the light colored shells bring light into the pond so it can be seen better by the passing admirer—fairy or human. When you are done, add water carefully to the pond.

I like to place my gardens in an area where they will blend in naturally. This can be a challenge at times as you don't want the fairy garden to become too engulfed in the regular garden or outside landscaping. So take care in finding that perfect spot to admire your beautiful little fairy haven.

Chapter 3

A Mexican Fairy Garden

Did you know that there are fairies all over the world and each has adapted to its climactic conditions? Well, it's true! And because of this, a garden of cacti and succulents, red earth, and hot sun is not surprising for certain fairies to prefer, especially those living in desert environments.

If you happen to reside in a desert-like place (or simply prefer cacti to flowing greenery), have no fear. You, too, can create beautiful miniature gardens for your fairies to enjoy. Just follow these simple steps.

No fairy could be enticed to visit a garden that looks like this!

1. Select some small cacti and succulents from a local nursery.

2. For my succulent garden, I decided not to uproot my very sad cactus but to give it some surgery and fill the pot with fresh potting soil.

3. Arrange your small cacti or succulents around the back of the old cacti or succulents, as I did here, to create the illusion of a forest of cacti. This will also leave the front of your container free to embellish any way you choose. For my garden, I used the large white stones that had been in the pot already (waste not, want not!).

I even stuck in the bit of sick looking cactus I cut from the old plant in the hopes that it will eventually spring back to life.

4. Now you must add something to truly transform your pot of plants into a magical miniature garden. One easy way of doing this is adding a pathway for fairies to frolic down. For this I used colored sand bought at a craft store, but you can choose tiny pebbles, lichen, small stones, or other items.

5. If you still feel as if you are only looking at a pot with a bunch of cacti placed in it, you can add on to our garden by placing it near other cacti or succulents to give it a sort of backdrop. For my garden, I dragged in an ancient cactus my mother had for many years. I thought I would just pick it up and pop it down as a backdrop for my fairy garden, but the poor plant had outgrown its old pot! Sadly, this is where I dropped it because it was too prickly to hold.

I decided before I could use this plant in my cacti garden I had to repot it. Afterward, it looked much happier.

The repotted cactus was used to make a backdrop for my Mexican fairy garden. I also added an old oyster shell for a bit of textural interest. It has a bleached look that resembles weathered rock.

6. Now your garden should be more or less finished, ready for any hot weather fairy to come and enjoy. I have added a pergola type construction (the instructions will be in chapter 15) and bit of bark that was lying around, too.

And don't forget to find a fairy to add to your garden should you like!

The Succulent Garden

Succulents are a really fun plant to work with and help create a truly enchanted fairy oasis. As a child I had a potted pig-face and was always picking up the juicy round petals and planting them in other pots—it's a wonder my house wasn't overrun with them!

To propagate succulents, all you need to do is take one leaf and bury it in the dirt. Chain of Hearts was another favorite plant of mine as a child, and it was as equally easy to make new plants from as pig-face.

For a succulent garden, try using a wide, shallow dish or box for starters and then follow these steps and embellish when you feel like it!

- Add potting soil to your container and arrange the plants on the top before you actually dig them in.

2. You will also want some rocks to add to the container, to make a landscape around your plants.

3. Put in the plants.

4. Arrange the rocks so that they create an exciting environment for fairies to visit. If you have enough space and enough rocks, why not try creating a labyrinth for the fairies to navigate?

5. If you want to create a path, you can use any type of crushed rock, sand, pebbles, and the like. For a path I chose to use colored sand. I particularly like the colored sand for these warm climate gardens as it reminds me of the desert or the beach. But remember: if you use sand, your path may run a bit when your garden gets watered, so you may need to keep some extra sand on hand to help rebuild the path after watering.

Succulent fairy gardens actually make wonderful beach gardens for fairies to visit when they want to relax in the sun. I chose to make mine a beach garden as a nice contrast to the cacti garden. Shells are a great addition to any sand you place in your garden. Using the shells as a border will help keep your path intact during watering.

6. Shade is also necessary in the heat and a cute beach umbrella is just the right accessory to add to your succulent beach garden! You can either find store-bought umbrellas or simply collect a few drink umbrellas. In this case, I used plastic covers for drinks and they work wonderfully as fairy umbrellas.

Chapter 4

The Hanging Fairy Garden

Hanging baskets make excellent gardens and dwelling places for fairies. They are up out of the reach of animals, such as cats, and the fairies can enjoy the gentle swaying of their gardens in a sweet summer breeze. They can also be kept up out of frost and flood level, galumphing big boots, and lawn mowers. One hanging basket can be a very attractive addition to a garden but why not create several? You can link them up with rope ladders and walkways and call it a true fairy village!

You can make the baskets in such a village uniform by using baskets with coconut matting in a wire frame, solid plastic, or try a combination of whatever is lying around your shed or garage. You will need a suitable tree to hang your baskets from, so take care when choosing a good branch or trunk. Or you can get a metal shepherd's hook to hang in any place in your yard. I chose a tree in my yard, though I was somewhat worried about the roaming possums who visit us every night using that tree as a staircase to our roof. So do take care in choosing a good spot to hang your garden from. In my case, perhaps the fairies will tame these cute but noisy creatures and ride them like horses—preferably away from our roof.

The Spanish Chestnut Fairy Village

Here are some simple steps to create a hanging garden for your fairies to visit.

I. Select your hanging baskets. If you are not sure how many you can handle at first, start with one and build from there. I have chosen a new wire basket, an ancient wire basket, and a plastic hanging basket for my garden village. Fill all baskets with potting soil.

2. You now will need to choose plants suitable for surviving outside under the shaded canopy of the tree (or suited to whatever sun level they get based on where you hang the basket from). Do keep in mind you will have to keep these pots watered regularly and you will have to be able to reach them to do this. For hanging basket gardens, hardy plants will work best, especially if you think you won't manage enough waterings in a week.

3. Plant your selected foliage according to directions. Once everything is planted, you can now add the fairy accessories to make each basket attractive to fairies:

a cottage, a chair, paving, fences, and the like are all good ideas for hanging basket gardens.

4. Now you will need to hoist your lovely garden(s) up into a tree or onto a shepherd's hook.

5. We all know fairies can fly but sometimes they prefer to walk. If you are using multiple pots for your garden village, you will need to link the pots by various means. Make several of the rustic ladders I have designed and given instructions for in chapter 15. Or make a long mini Popsicle stick fence that can also be used as a walkway. Measure how long the distances are between the pots once you've hung them up. This will help you when creating the walkways for your fairies.

Another item you can use is plastic netting typically used for packaging fruit. These make great hammocks for fairies as well.

To give added flare to your hanging gardens, try to purchase some tiny solar-powered garden lights and let the magic shine!

Chapter 5

The Renovated/ Rescued Fairy Garden

Not all fairy gardens need to be made from scratch. Why not revamp that messy or neglected corner of your yard or garden and make it into your own enchanted wonderland? The more sheltered and secret the area is, the better for attracting fairies. Make use of the existing plants in the area and then add embellishments to create a fairy's paradise.

This is also especially good if you don't have a particularly green thumb or if you are too busy to tend to a larger garden but have plants that need some perking up. Personally, I have always thought I would love to be a gardener. Unfortunately, I never have the time to do all the upkeep necessary to having a flourishing garden. This means I have lots of parts of my garden and yard that need rescuing or renovating. And fairy gardening is the perfect way to perk them up!

For the first of these projects I chose a big pot that was sitting on my patio. It contains a lime tree one of my brothers gave me a few Christmases ago.

To create a fairy garden from an existing potted plant, follow these directions:

1. The first step is to weed the pot (that's fairly straightforward)!

2. Next, top up the dirt with fresh potting soil.

In my case, there were numerous hanging pots all in various states of disrepair hanging along the patio railing. The one sitting directly above the potted lime plant was just the thing for two Polyanthus. If you have other parts of your yard or hanging baskets that need a little sprucing up, adding a small flower or plant and a few fairy items will give it the boost it needs.

3. Potted plants are great places to add water features. A pond is something all fairies need. The one in the following photo was a homemade pottery effort that had a great rustic look to it. The terracotta tile was bought from a fairy garden store on eBay.

(I wasn't sure about actually planting other plants in the same pot as the lime in case I killed it or the other plants, so I left it alone for a while. Instead, I added two little miniature Popsicle stick gates, as well as three of my champagne wire chairs (instructions are given in chapter 15). To my delight, a fairy came to visit shortly after!)

4. The next step was to add paving stones. I had bought some cork squares with adhesive backing that were perfect for the job. Isabelle stopped by and thought that the fairy needed to go back to see if she liked the changes I had made. Make sure to place your fairy in the garden once in a while when you are creating it so you can get a good sense of whether you need more additions or if it's nearing completion.

The wonderful thing about fairy gardens—and repurposed ones at that—is that you can always add or detract things to your liking. For example, with the above garden, the next morning I decided it looked empty. It needed some ground covering. Moss would have been nice, but I didn't have any, so I used a bag of smooth river pebbles instead. This made the garden look much more inviting.

I still wanted something extra in it, though. I realized I needed to tie in the upper hanging basket to the lime tree pot garden and for that I needed a ladder. I used cotoneaster twigs and raffia to make a suitable ladder (instructions are given in chapter 15).

I also didn't like the Popsicle stick gates after seeing them again so I replaced them with a wreath made of cotoneaster to look a bit like an archway. To make this type of archway, you need a length of cotoneaster and then form a loop with it. Wind the tail in and out round the loop until finished. I was happy with this effect and finally felt that my garden was complete. It may take you a few days or even weeks to achieve the right look and feel to your renovated or revived garden but once you have it just right, you'll find new excuses to be out in your yard and tending your fairy garden.

Chapter 6

Impromptu Fairy Gardens

I know a bank where the wild thyme blows,
Where oxlips and the nodding violet grows,
Quite over-canopied with luscious woodbine,
With sweet musk-roses and with eglantine:
There sleeps Titania some time of the night,
Lull'd in these flowers with dances and delight;
And there the snake throws her enamell'd skin,
Weed wide enough to wrap a fairy in.

—William Shakespeare, *A Midsummer Night's Dream*

Sometimes you might need to make a garden in a hurry. Or perhaps the opportunity arises and you decide you'd like to turn something ordinary into something magical. How can you make a fabulous fairy garden on the spot with little or no preparation? This chapter will show you how to make something wonderful virtually out of nothing. And it all begins with flowers. Flowers, picked and placed in decorative patterns, are an easy way to form an impromptu garden. However, if there are no flowers around, you can use leaves, twigs, and any other available greenery for your garden. Consider picking up pebbles, pine cones, seed pods, fallen birds' nests, shells, feathers, or even bits of colored plastic like bottle caps to use in your garden.

In Australia, where I live, there is a native bird called a Satin Bowerbird and one of the peculiarities of the male bird is to collect blue colored ephemera with which to adorn his lovely grassy bower in order to attract a female. And just like the Satin Bowerbird, fairies, too, are attracted by pretty and glittery things if they are arranged properly, so keep this in mind when creating any of your fairy gardens, but particularly those impromptu gardens.

Wild Flower Garden

The types of flowers you use in this garden will depend on the country and area in which you live in. If you are in North America or Canada, the United Kingdom, or Northern Europe, you will have quite different flowers than those found in the Mediterranean or the tropics.

Here in Australia our wild flowers tend to be small, delicate, and often grown in clusters. We also have some imported plants that have gone wild, sometimes to the point of being classified as noxious weeds. But even these can make a charming fairy garden.

To make an impromptu garden you can use whatever is in your vicinity, whether native or a weed. Simply follow these directions and improvise with whatever you have around you:

- Clear the area of clutter, such as stray twigs and leaves. You can also put these aside to be used later.

2. Look around for flowers.

3. Begin arranging the flowers you've found. Try placing them in circles, semicircles, or parallel rows to mimic the formal beds of large country house gardens.

4. Once you have your flower pattern established, you can also line the flower path with pebbles.

5. Find rocks or pieces of bark to make into furniture for your garden.

6. Now all you need is a fairy to visit!

Home-Style Garden

If you are searching for an activity to keep your children occupied, then there is nothing nicer than spending the afternoon in the garden making little places for fairies to come visit. Of course, this pastime is not solely for children, as playing in the yard or garden can be fun for people of all ages! So embrace your inner child when making the home-style garden.

1. Search for a suitable spot for your impromptu garden. Make sure it is not a spot being used regularly or one that will interfere with normal gardening activities.

2. Clear fallen debris, twigs, and branches that are in the way. Put all these trimmings and pieces aside as they can be used in fashioning furniture for your miniature garden.

3. Again, just as you did for the wild flower garden, see what plants you can find and repurpose close to the spot you've chosen for your fairy garden. My garden pictured here is very simple and consists of things that are in my yard nearly all year round.

4. You can also build up your garden to have multiple tiers. I've taken a log from the wood pile to help build different levels to my garden. You might also use rocks if you have any to create this effect. Use the differences tiers to create a couple of focal points for your fairy garden. Place flowers on the upper level so that it acts as a kind of patio or lookout point for one of your fairies.

5. Make the lower level as attractive as the upper, but this time use darker or bigger flowers if you have any to increase the sense of depth.

6. Now you must to link the two areas to finish this multilayered garden effect. You can do this by making a path of flowers from the bottom level up the log or other barrier to the higher one.

7. Whether you have a path of flowers leading up the log or not, you should consider adding a rustic ladder—one perfect for a fairy to climb while resting her wings. Instructions for this are given in chapter 15.

8. If you have leftover twigs from clearing away your fairy garden space, here is a good idea of what you can use them for. Freshly cut twigs (in my case, from cotoneaster) are very pliable and can be twisted to form little wreaths that can then be used as windows or hanging swings.

9. Play around with your garden and its accessories until you are satisfied with the positioning of everything. If you've created a swing, see if you can catch a fairy swinging in your garden the next time you visit.

How to Make a Clover Chain

As a child I spent hours sitting in the grass chatting with friends while we each attempted to make the longest clover chain we could. We'd run home to lunch swathed in streams of wilting clover flowers and very sticky green fingers. You, too, can easily create clover chains to adorn your fairy gardens (or just your heads):

1. Find a patch of clover (watch out for bees!) or buy some from the garden center.

2. Pick two clover flowers with long stems.

3. Make a slit in the stem of one flower, somewhere along its middle.

4. Slide the other clover flower into the slit and pull until the flower head is snug against the stem of the first one.

5. Now, make a slit in the stem of the flower you have just slipped into the first stem and repeat the process with a third clover flower.

6. Continue this process until your chain is to a desired length.

Try this method with other flowers and make sure the heads of the flowers are close together. Also add some leaves to get a different effect. Use the chains for personal adornment or to drape over your fairy gardens. They won't last forever but can be a fun weekly addition to your garden.

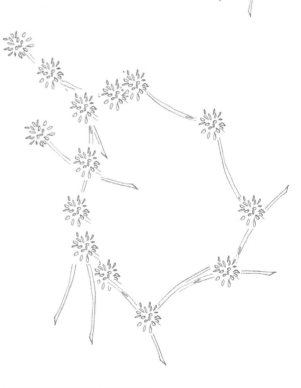

Chapter 7

The Fernery

Cool, green, elegant ferns—nothing can be more inviting on a hot summer's day. Ferns of all varieties and sizes can be purchased at your local nursery or garden center. Many are easy to grow and just need the right conditions in which to thrive for years and years. My mother has always owned a maiden hair fern and it is possible that the current one is a descendent of one she planted many years ago.

The Ferny Dell

This garden would do well in either a terrarium or in a shady corner of your yard or patio. You will need a variety of small ferns to construct this miniature garden. If it is to be an outside garden, then you will need plants that can survive outside and tolerate a range of temperatures and weather conditions. If you don't want to worry about the outside upkeep of such a garden, a terrarium is a good option and is the kind I decided to use here.

1. Prepare your terrarium (as per the specific instructions for a terrarium) or garden corner by building up with potting soil. For an outdoor garden, some rocks will make a nice border around your ferny garden.

2. Arrange your ferns how you would like them. For a natural look you will find the larger ones go well at the back of the garden and then the smaller ones immediately in front of them.

3. This is a dell and that means that it should not all be on one level. Before you plant the ferns build up the back part of the garden with extra potting soil. Remember, though, that the soil will run when watered, so I suggest using some rocks to build a retaining wall. Then you are ready to plan your ferns.

4. When planting ferns, you want to have handy a good-sized watering can full of water to help the ferns settle after being taken out of their pots.

5. For my garden, I decided to use a few more rocks of varying sizes to make this look like a natural ferny dell in miniature. If you can get rocks with their own moss attached, the effect will be even better.

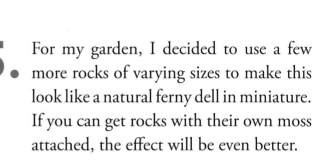

6. Ferns live in places where there is a lot of fallen leaf matter to mulch into the soil. To get this effect in your terrarium or outside garden, you can use sphagnum moss and it will give an extra mossy look to your enchanted garden.

7. Think about adding some paving stones for extra effect. But you must consider the environment you've created with the ferns and choose your type of paving stones wisely. I personally think shells would be inappropriate here as you are aiming for your garden to look rather rustic and natural. Pebbles would be a good option in this case. Make the path go in and out of the ferns to suggest that under the foliage there are possible fairy dwellings.

This type of garden calls for subtlety so keep to the colors suggested by the plants and moss. A wire champagne chair would suit this garden, because of the delicate wire frame and the lichen backing. Or you can insert a twig chair as long as it isn't too big and dominating. Even try a simple four poster bed with torn lace canopy for a perfect fairy napping place. I bet a fairy would love a take a rest in such a peaceful and magical spot.

Chapter 8

Wild Fairy Gardens

Up the airy mountain,
Down the rushy glen,
We daren't go a-hunting
For fear of little men;
Wee folk, good folk,
Trooping all together;
Green jacket, red cap,
And white owl's feather!

—William Allingham, *The Fairies*

There are places away from civilization that would make the most perfect fairy garden. Go out into the yard or the forest and fashion a garden from fallen twigs and moss-covered stumps that will attract fairies with an extra rustic charm.

Fairies are shy creatures and many of them are too frightened to venture into urban areas. You will still find, though, if you are very quiet and careful, evidence of fairies in less populated areas. They love woods and forests, boulders covered in moss, and shady fern-filled glens. These places often look like fabulous gardens already. Sometimes they require just a hint of something extra to make them into an extra special fairy garden.

My most favorite place in the world is the Pine Forest, which is just out of my hometown of Armidale, New South Wales, Australia. It was planted in the 1920s with radiata pine to be harvested for timber. It never has been properly used for its intended purpose, though, but instead it has become a popular spot for local residents who walk their dogs, ride their horses and mountain bikes, re-enact medieval battles, and go for picnics.

Living in Australia—but with strong British sensibilities—the Pine Forest gives us a touch of that old-world European feel and it is inevitable that fairies who emigrated to Australia with British settlers will also find it a suitable home away from home.

Stump Castle Garden

An old stump can make a perfect fairy garden. Particularly, old stumps of pine trees look like the ruins of old castles, and this will be my inspiration for this rustic fairy garden:

1. Clear around the stump and remove anything that makes it look messy.

2. If you can, make a clear path from the ground up to the draw-bridge or door of the "castle."

3. Use pine cones, bits of wood, and twigs to make the castle look as though it has doors and windows.

4. Now it's time to create the garden that will complement the castle. Gather moss, lichen, little flowers, leaves, stones, and anything that is interesting to the eye, and begin to decorate the castle.

5. I just happened to have two spare fairies in my pocket, so I placed them in my garden. They put everything into scale and become the focal point for everything in the garden. Remember, it's important that each fairy garden you create has a focal point, whether it's a piece of furniture, a water feature, a particular miniature plant, or simply a tiny fairy.

Chapter 9

Of Moss, Lichen, and Fungi

Grey lichens, mid they hills of creeping thyme,
Grow like to fairy forests hung with rime;
And fairy money-pots are often found
That spring like little mushrooms out of ground,
Some shaped like cups and some in slender trim
Wine glasses like, that to the very rim
Are filled with little mystic shining seed.
—John Clare, *Fairy Things*

Nothing seems to conjure up an image of fairyland like green moss growing on a boulder in a shady glade dotted with beautiful toadstools. Lichen hanging from the branches of ancient apple trees looks as though it is fairyland's wrought iron.

This chapter will discuss these three plant types, how and where to obtain them, and the possibilities of growing your own as well as how to use them in your magical miniature gardens.

We shall start with that luxuriously soft and springy substance: moss. If you peer around the cooler side of your house or in a wooded area—especially if you live in a colder and/or moist climate—you will most likely find clumps of what resembles green pillows growing here and there at the base of the foundation or at the bottoms of rocks and trees. This is a common type of moss and one that you can raid to put into your fairy gardens. You might also find it growing on bricks that are also shaded from the sun. If you are very lucky you may live in a climate that encourages moss to spread widely and it may even be used as a lawn substitute.

To grow moss you will need to collect some from one of these domestic sources or go out into the wild to see what you can find (you may also find certain types of moss at your local garden center). You will need to give the moss a suitable place in which to grow—damp, cool, and sheltered. You really will find it hard to speed the growth of moss and the best you can do is to help it along by keeping it moist.

I have also found moss in our local pine forest. Trees that have rotted and fallen to the ground, and are kept in a perpetually moist and cool environment, are often covered in moss. I have collected samples and brought them home and kept them successfully in a shaded plastic container with lots of water. There are suggestions for potions that can be concocted and applied to a surface in order to encourage the growth of moss, but I can't guarantee that any of these will work sufficiently.

Another method you can try for growing moss is to scratch around on a cool, moist part of the garden, removing all the grass and weeds. Push the clumps of gathered moss into the area and keep it well watered. Sphagnum moss will probably be easier to buy at a garden center than grow unless you live close to a peat bog.

Lichen, the next on our list, is actually a composite of two plants growing symbiotically (or in other words, together as one). You can try to grow your own lichen, but it is a tricky thing to do and you are probably better off looking in the woods for some that is growing naturally. The lichen I have used in various gardens loves to grow on old and dead trees. The lichen resembles disintegrating lacey curtains and is great for the backs of champagne wire chairs, fairy pillows, and also in artificial gardens.

Fungi, the last on our list, are also easy to find in the wild, depending on your climate. I haven't used real fungi in my fairy gardens yet, but there is no reason you couldn't try doing so. Again, you will need to duplicate the environment where you find the fungi in order for it to grow successfully in your garden, and this can be a rather difficult task.

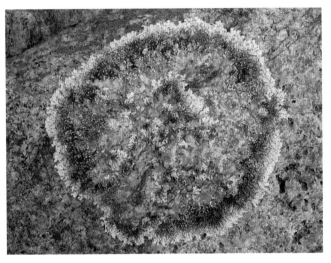

Remember that moss, lichen, and fungi replicate by sending out spores, so you will need to have a specimen that is on the point of doing this. I suggest that the easiest way to grow fungi is to gather living plants with their environment attached—such as a fallen tree branch or a clump of earth. You will also find there are different types of fungi growing in your own backyard. I found a lovely example of an orange fungus growing out of a log on our wood pile one day. It had been raining heavily for a few days, followed by a nice warm sunny day, and the next thing I knew, this gorgeous fungus sprang up.

If you find it difficult to find a fungus in the wild that you'd like to add to your garden, you can simply purchase a commercially available mushroom farm and see what fungi will grow out of that.

A note of caution: Be careful about handling fungi and other plants that you don't know much about. They could be poisonous to touch and especially to eat. This can be said of many plants, actually, so always be cautious and use common sense when handling plants or fungi you are unfamiliar with.

Chapter 10

Magic Corners and Shady Nooks

While you may have already renovated a corner of your yard or garden, this chapter will provide you with tips on how to make tiny gardens in those forgotten places in your larger garden or yard: beneath the brickwork, inside the honeysuckle, down beside the vegetable garden—all can be places that might attract fairies.

What Can a Chair Do?

This project is so simple you'll want to do it over and over. Take a twig chair, four poster bed, or champagne wire chairs. Grab a fairy or two and whatever else you would like to use in a fairy garden. Go out into the yard and start finding little corners to place these items in. Take photos or just leave them there as secrets to be found by the fairies or, perhaps, curious children.

Behind the Trash Cans

Normally trash cans are not considered a romantic, whimsical, or very nice place, but you never know where a perfect area for a mini garden might crop up. For me, there was something attractive about the cement block wall with ivy growing up it and the foreground of long juicy dandelion leaves in my yard. I had twin pots that I wanted to use together for a garden and so I decided this was the perfect spot for it. To recreate a garden similar to mine, here are the very simple steps:

1. Place the twin pots side by side. Mine had been outside waiting for me to turn them into fairy gardens and I'm afraid they got a bit messy. But never mind—they will soon be filled with potting soil!

2. Plant the pots with tree-like plants (you can find miniature versions of trees and shrubs at your local garden center that are perfect for the job) that will like a good amount shade (or sun, if your special spot gets abundant sunshine). For my two pots, I planted hebe in one and two dwarf box in the other.

3. Consider adding a tiny house between the box bushes.

4. Take a Popsicle stick picket fence (instructions given in chapter 15) and balance it across from pot to pot as a type of walkway.

5. Add a terracotta terrace and a shell path.

6. Then try some different effects and accessories to flush out your truly magical garden, and don't forget your fairy!

Chapter 11

Logs and Other Unusual Containers

Beautiful ceramic pots can make delightful and whimsical gardens, but why not try something a little a little out of the ordinary as a container for your fairy garden? Old suitcases, baskets, tins, and whatever else you can dream up can all be transformed into something wonderful and magical for your miniature garden.

One of the delights of creating a fairy garden is finding all sorts of unusual containers to make them out of. Gardens can be made from all sorts of things—although, depending on where you want to put your garden and how long you want it to last, there will be some restrictions.

First, you need to consider the way water will drain from your container. For plants to thrive, they cannot be too dry or too wet. If possible, make sure there are sufficient drainage holes in the base of whatever container you decide to use. If necessary you might need to drill (or ask an adult to help, if a child is creating the garden) to put half a dozen small holes in the base of your container.

Durability of your garden holder is another issue you must consider before constructing your garden. Certain materials will decay quicker than others and therefore have to be sheltered from the elements or just left to melt back into the earth. If you choose a material that will decay, be prepared to replace it over time.

What Kinds of Containers Can Be Used?

You can use almost anything you like (with proper drainage holes) to contain your fairy garden. An old suitcase is certainly unusual and will be a talking point of any garden. It will fall apart with rain, however, especially once filled with earth. If you want to try using an old suitcase from either your basement, closet, or a thrift store, insert a plastic lining inside before filling with soil (like a pond lining or a sheet used in landscaping), but still make sure there are drainage holes in both the lining and the suitcase. The lining will, hopefully, increase the life of the garden and the container.

An old, rusty wheelbarrow is another interesting and inviting fairy garden holder. These are often used in garden decoration so can easily be used for fairy gardens. Old wheelbarrows may have rust spots in the bottom for drainage already, but you may need to drill a few extra holes, depending on the size and what types of plants you choose to include in the planter.

A Log Garden

If you live in a climate that gets decidedly chilly in winter, you may have a fireplace and you may also have a wood pile. If that's the case, you may find some fairly standard-sized logs that can be used to help construct an interesting and rustic-looking fairy garden. Here is one that I created from logs. You can modify as suits your needs.

1. Choose a couple of interesting looking logs from the wood pile and look for somewhere suitable in the garden to place them. I wanted a moist, mossy type of garden so I chose our ivy-covered wall as a backdrop. Arrange your logs into a pleasing composition and one that won't easy fall over.

2. Now, you must begin playing with elements that you want in your garden. I decided to try adding a rustic ladder first.

3. Once you are ready, add a little potting soil to your logs. You will need to add it carefully or you will get a very messy garden. Dampen it down with a trickle of water, pressing lightly to compact the soil.

4. Now it's time to add some plants. For my garden, I decided to start by adding moss. The moss was homegrown from a long-neglected pot that had been left in a moist shady corner of the yard. I also added a trailing plant. This one pictured is a fine-leafed Myoporum that will

eventually have small white flowers on it when it blooms. This trailing plant may need to be replaced as it really prefers a bit more sun, but it also likes well-drained soil and is frost tolerant.

5. Next, choose some paving stones to add. For my garden, I used small light colored pebbles.

6. The logs might not look quite like a fairy garden yet. So, try adding a plastic swing (as I did) from a cheap doll house set bought at a thrift store—or other accessory to your liking.

7. As my garden still looked a bit empty, I tried adding two salt and pepper shaker mushrooms that I've had since the 1970s. The effect was quite wacky. I liked it, but my granddaughter thought it looked a bit corny. In any case, finding vintage kitchenware or dolls' house items are a wonderful way to dress up your fairy garden. You never know what might work well!

8. If you tire of one item in your garden, feel free to replace it. In my case, I removed the plastic swing and added a fairy chair and an old bird's nest.

9. The key to a successful fairy garden is having a balanced composition, and this can be tricky if you are using found objects, such as uneven logs. I encountered such a problem with this garden. One end of the horizontal log was too abruptly angled. It needed a gentle slope of potting soil leading up to it to help add better balance.

10. I also added another Myoporum to balance the greenery.

11. As you work with your garden, you may find you need additional items or to expand what you already have placed in the garden. More paving stones were needed for the fairies to climb up from the ground onto the raised log in my garden, so I added a few more.

12. Keep adding and taking away items as you see fit. As you can see, my garden has evolved (there are no more mushrooms, for example, but the chair remained).

13.

After a bit of fiddling, you will finally have a successful garden. I settled on two fairy chairs and a pergola-type structure (instructions are given in chapter 15). The absolute finishing touch was some flowers from an ornamental peach tree that I made into little garden beds on the log. And voila! A lovely fairy garden made out of ordinary old logs. Creating a garden from found objects can be a labor of love—but quite rewarding and also inexpensive!

Old Metal Toolbox Garden

A friend of mine started making a fairy garden but after planting it she didn't know where to go from there. She gave me the old metal toolbox that she had bought at the Dump Shop (the rubbish shop near our home). Her method for putting in drainage holes was rather unorthodox but effective, yet I don't recommend it as a general rule. Instead of drilling the holes with an electric drill she bashed the holes into the bottom of the case with the claw head of a hammer. If you don't have an electric drill but you have a hammer, be sure to get a large heavy duty nail and a block of wood that will fit snugly under the upside down metal case. Hit the nail with the hammer through the metal to make drainage holes. Put in about five of them before you start working on your garden.

The following are basic steps for creating a fairy garden out of a metal toolbox.

1. Once you've drilled in drainage holes at the bottom of the toolbox, add in potting soil. Then you can add some plants. As I had inherited this garden from my friend, it already had some plants growing in it. However, it had been in my garden for a few weeks waiting for me to attend to it. When it came to me it had small, newly planted plants in it but when I finally got to working on it, they were growing rampant! This is not a bad thing to work with, however, and will make the garden look more mature.

2. The lid of a toolbox container, especially an old one, might very difficult to open all the way, so it might be a challenge to get certain plants or other items into the container. But think of a rusty old lid as a rock overhang especially with the moss and luxurious plant growth. One would expect to find worn old logs in an environment like this so you may decide to add a few wooden items in to give it this effect. I used my plastic aquarium bridge to help hold down the mint that was planted in the garden.

When I bought the aquarium bridge, I also couldn't resist this artificial weathered log. It makes a good natural-looking bridge from the ground up to the plateau of the toolbox. I have also added a tiny resin house on top of the moss for added detail. Use your imagination and let it run wild!

3. As with the other gardens we've discussed, keep adding and removing items as you see fit. I inserted one of my champagne wire chairs (instructions given in chapter 15) onto the bridge. The back of the garden was rather dark and a bit indistinct, so I placed a mini Popsicle stick picket fence along the hinge area to lighten it up (instructions for fence given in chapter 15).

Your final garden is sure to be whimsical and unique—and to invite all sorts of fairies into your little oasis.

Chapter 12

Artificial Fairy
Gardens

erhaps you are concerned that you aren't blessed with a green thumb and wonder how you can possibly make a fairy garden—and keep it flourishing. Well, don't let that stop you from making the most exquisite gardens to attract fairies to your home! Fairy gardens can also be made from artificial plants and other materials and make just as nice (and everlasting) miniature gardens for fairy visitors.

Artificial Suitcase Garden

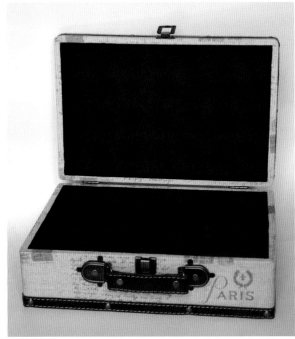

I adore old-fashioned suitcases, especially those that have travel stickers on them. Take a trip to your local thrift or antique store and search for the perfect suitcase for your artificial fairy garden. I found this little gem at a local shop that sells all sorts of interesting (and mainly decorative) items.

I couldn't bring myself to fill the lovely clean interior with real potting soil (besides, I would have had to drill holes in the bottom for drainage and that would have destroyed the case as well), so I decided I'd use this case for an artificial fairy garden.

As I was planning out my garden, I thought back to my daughter's childhood when she was a fan of the Polly Pocket toys. In the late 1980s Polly Pocket had very small travel cases that weren't much bigger than a powder compact. When opened the lid and the base formed a perfect vignette for Polly to live in. The ones I loved best often had a pool and slide, sun umbrella, and a fern or two in the yard. So that was my inspiration for my artificial fairy garden in my suitcase. You may be inspired by something else but here are some easy steps to creating your own timeless (and hassle-free) artificial magical garden.

1. Line your suitcase with some kind of turf-type material. I contemplated using velvet or green paper but then remembered that I had bought meters of a special flock paper for my son years ago. The paper was a bit battered and creased but that only made it look more natural. You may want to use actual artificial sod or packing materials or anything that suits your fancy.

After tracing around the base of the box to get the right proportions for the turf, I cut the paper so that it covered the base and the four sides of the body of the case with a bit left to cover over the hinges of the lid. Then I glued it into place.

2. Now all the hard work had been done and the fun could begin. The beauty of this kind of garden is that it doesn't have to stay the same forever, unless you really want all the pieces glued into place. To start, I put in four artificial potted plants.

Then I couldn't resist putting a couple more on the outside of the case, to add to the overall ambiance of the garden setting.

3. Next I pulled a potted jade plant (a real one) over to the left and added an apple topiary tree I'd found at a secondhand shop on the hinged ledge of the suitcase.

I'd been fiddling around with trying to make picket fences from assorted craft supplies and put a fence in the case just under the apple topiary. I also added a couple of artificial bonsais, one in each front corner of the case. The beauty of the artificial garden is that you can add whatever you like and have a little more freedom to move items around as you see fit.

4. Next came two little doll house chairs, and I quite liked the pink against the black of the inside of the case lid. I also added a mini artist's canvas on an easel which stood ready for the fairy painter to make a masterpiece.

All finished!

5. After a while, I removed the easel and put up an archway made of two pieces of artificial wheat I'd made by twisting them together with florists wire.

6. Still not content (and you may find yourself in the same predicament), I removed the fence, the fairies, and the apple tree. Clearing one side of the case and rearranging the artificial trees on the other, I then lay down some pebbles around the edges. I decided to add a pond to my suitcase garden.

7. If you feel that the top of the case is making your garden too dark, you may want to add a picture of a garden or forest or something to brighten it up. I chose a photo I had taken of the pine forest near my town. I printed the picture out on photographic paper using my own printer. If you don't have a suitable photo, you can use an old calendar or magazine picture instead.

8. If you want to add the illusion of water to your artificial garden, consider using small blue acrylic stones from a craft shop. These are used mostly for vases but they make a great pond or stream for your fairy garden.

9. Consider adding a fence and other odds and ends to dress it up. Try various pieces that you have lying around the house (as I did with this aquarium bridge, which was just a tad too big) until you have exactly what you like.

10. I tried adding a fairy sitting on the shore of her own private pool.

11. Then I added a tiny outhouse in one corner, but it could also be used as a shed or changing room for the pond.

Artificial fairy gardens are great gifts or activities to make for children's birthday parties. You can simply provide a friend with a suitcase (either lining it with some sort of felt or other artificial turf or including it in the package), add a jar of blue acrylic stones, a couple of artificial potted plants, a small bag of pebbles, a picket fence, and a fairy. Then present the whole package as a birthday present. This should keep anyone out of mischief for hours!

Another Suitcase Garden

Even though I was pleased with the results of my first suitcase garden I had so much fun I decided to redecorate it after a while—this is the beauty of an artificial garden; you can change it whenever you desire! I left the artificial turf (the type used for model railways) inside as I had glued it in. I wanted a different backdrop, though—something softer and more handmade looking than the photograph I had originally chosen. I found some scrapbooking paper I'd bought that looked like faded manuscripts. One of these had a window picture on it and it suited the idea of an indoor suitcase garden looking out into the world.

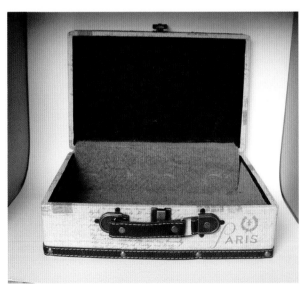

Here is what I did next so that you could also replicate a garden similar to this.

1. Cut the paper to fit the lid of the box and try to fit the picture in it. You may have to cut it out in sections and paste it so that the design matches up. Glue into place.

2. Add some topiary to the case to fit the formal look of the window.

3. Add two champagne wire chairs.

4. Add other bits and pieces. I chose ceramic frogs sitting on leaves. They are so realistic and a little bit bizarre. Frogs can make good fairy pets.

 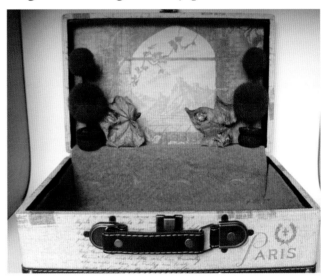

5. I then tried out a simple Popsicle stick and cardboard bed.

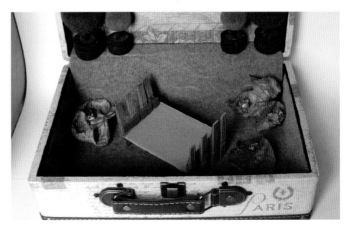

6. I removed those and then added lace drapery to add mystery and texture to the garden.

7. Add the two artificial bonsais.

8. The garden is taking on the appearance of a lovely fairy bathroom in a way, based on the items I've chosen to include inside.

9. Adding a pebble floor makes it feel as if the outdoors has been brought inside.

10. And finished! It's just right for two small fairy girls!

Wooden Box with Fairy Garden Mini Kit

As birthdays or holidays approach, you may decide that a fairy doll in a box with her own plants and accessories might make a nice present for a fairy-loving friend or a child. And this can be accomplished with just a simple container and a few accessories.

The wooden box I show here is from a secondhand shop and must have been decorated in the past as it had blobs of paint on it that had been scraped off. This effect made it lookcd aged. If you are looking for something a little more decorative, many gift and thrift shops have cardboard gift boxes shaped like books. These are ideal for making a similar mini fairy garden kit for a gift or for a birthday party project. Here is what you need:

1. A wooden box or similar container with a few accessories (I chose fairy chairs).

2. Include some fake topiary and moss-covered boulders.

3. Include a few fairies, too, so the gift receiver can choose which to include in their fairy garden.

4. Cut out suitable paper and glue to the front if desired.

5. Cut out something pretty for the inside as well, if desired.

6. Try different combinations of fairies and accessories until you have the perfect pairing of fairies and accessories.

7. Try to find accessories that match to your chosen fairy. For example, this tree will fit into the box and the fairy's dress fits the delicate inside finish of the box, too.

In the end, I had to remove the chair I had chosen because it wouldn't fit well and the fairy was too tiny to sit in it.

8. Standing on her mossy boulder next to her little tree, this fairy fits nicely into the box and is ready for wrapping up as a present.

A Child's Delight

This is another great activity for children to do, especially if it is wet or cold outside. It is a versatile project and can be used for birthday parties or any rainy day activity.

Find a shallow box. The one I chose came from the green grocer and had displayed fruit in it. I like the black uniformity of it. You can paint the box first if you want using basic acrylic paint (used with water for thinning and cleaning).

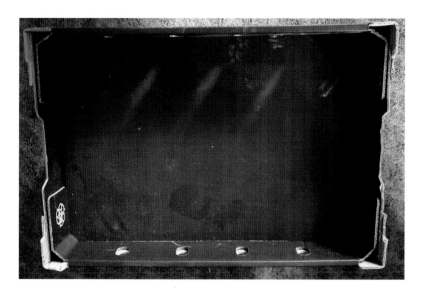

Cover the bottom of the box with colored paper if you haven't painted it. We used sheets from a scrapbooking pad. You may want to glue the paper in but we didn't because Izzy wanted to be able to change the look of her garden whenever she liked.

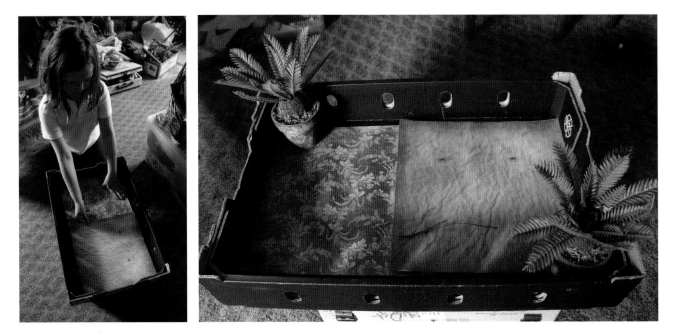

Insert your plants. The first plants Izzy put in were these two wonderful artificial palms with their rustic looking pots. She placed them in opposite corners of the box.

Add fake flowers for more color. The silk and plastic potted flowers were very popular and Izzy would have liked to use them all. She also chose an artificial bonsai for added effect.

It took quite a long time to decide what to put in next. A fake topiary tree and some real bark was one option. Izzy had trouble quite knowing what to do with these but she knew she wanted to use them. At the forefront there was a ceramic leaf with a frog on it propped against the log. And she added a chair so fairies can sit and enjoy their garden.

Adding topiaries is a nice way to imply tall trees for the fairy garden. Izzy had one with large apples on it. A couple of artificial moss-covered boulders were allowed to find their own place in the garden and the single chair was given a few friends.

Keep adding or taking away items as you or your child desire. Some more artificial plants went into Izzy's garden. She said that she wanted her garden to look like an enchanted forest. And in the end, she added two fairies to come and admire it.

Chapter 13

Fairy Terrariums

Fairy gardens in glass bowls may not afford the occupant a lot of privacy but they can be delightful enough that your fairy won't mind if human eyes watch her dancing in the garden. And terrarium fairy gardens are perfect for keeping inside all year round!

Giving Your Terrarium Garden a Natural Look

Finding the right glass bowl to house your inside fairy garden can be difficult. But once you find the right bowl, you'll be ready to go! Bowls can be expensive, however, so if you don't have much spare change left over to buy plants, you can certainly scavenge for plants around the yard or house to add to your garden.

For this garden, I found some charcoal, sphagnum moss, and potting soil around the house. The charcoal helps absorb odors resulting from water and vegetable matter being in a confined place. There is no drainage in a terrarium, so charcoal is a must-have ingredient.

Here are instructions for creating your own magical mini terrarium garden, perfect for a house fairy's visit:

1. Put a good layer of gravel or small pebbles in the bottom of your bowl.

2. Add a thin layer of charcoal.

3. Next, add your sphagnum moss or any other kind of moss. This layer is to help stop the potting mixture from falling down through the charcoal and pebbles and making it look dirty when viewed from the outside.

4. Finally add the potting soil. While you need enough to make your plants happy and able to thrive, you don't want too much to make the terrarium look as though it were simply full of potting soil and nothing else.

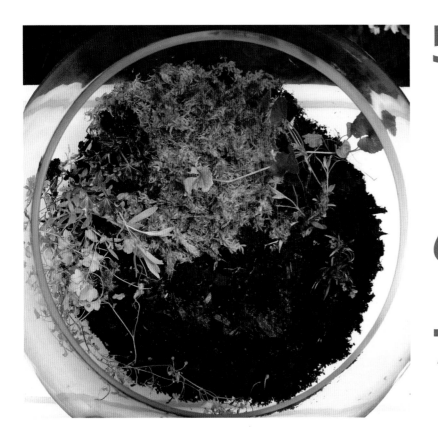

5. Then add the plants and flowers. For my terrarium, I looked through my outside garden to see what I could find. First, I found some small white violets and dug a couple of roots of them out.

6. Next to the violets was a pretty silvery ground cover that has white flowers, so I decided to add this too.

7. Bluebells can also be a nice addition and grow quite full once watered well.

8. Place your chosen plants to the sides of the pot and build up a mound of sphagnum moss toward the back. This will create the illusion of a hill.

Try adding in a bridge or other walkway feature as a focal point. My bridge was too big, unfortunately, so I inserted a small resin house on top of the mound and placed shells to form a path leading from it.

9. Consider adding a water feature or pond to your terrarium. You can use a shell for the bottom. I also chose to place a lovely mossy piece of bark near the front of the bowl.

10. Rocks and pieces of bark can add a nice rustic look to your terrarium fairy garden. I had been collecting rocks and pieces of bark with moss on them for a while and was storing them in a bucket with water in it to keep them moist. Rocks and pieces of mossy bark make nice rocky outcroppings behind the house (or other features you have included).

11. Then put in the finishing touches. I added a few more shells to make more of a paved area, a ceramic leaf with its own frog, and a fairy.

Chapter 14

Miscellaneous Fairy Gardens

There are all sorts of gardens that can be transformed into fairy gardens. The following projects do not fit into any particular category but are rather inspiration for creating a similar garden for your fairies. The thing to remember is: you cannot mess up a fairy garden, no matter how hard you try!

Lavender and Petunia Special

While I was hunting for spare pots in my garden shed, I discovered a couple of large pots that had never been used. Thinking it was time to remedy that, I hauled out this beautiful terracotta-colored plastic one and made ready to create a lovely fairy garden for my patio. To replicate this garden, follow these simple steps (and add your own flare where decided):

1. Fill the pot with potting soil.

2. Place your selected plants onto the top of the pot to see if the arrangement will work. Mine was going to be a simple planting: lavender in the middle surrounded by petunias and pansies on the outside.

I planted the lavender first as close to the middle as possible.

3. Place the other flowers around the middle flower (in this case, the lavender) as evenly as possible and arrange the colors so they either alternate or are grouped by hue.

4. Now your basic planted pot is done.

(Author's note: Now I have to confess that this lovely pot of flowers sat on my patio just like that for several weeks. During that time at least two of the pansies died for no apparent reason. The lavender got over its wilting and the petunias grew like wild fire. It was time to finally transform it into a fairy garden.)

5. Establish pathways for your fairies to navigate the garden. In such a jungle of a place how would the fairies find their way around? I thought a variety of different things would look good for this garden path and opted for pebbles and shells mainly.

Then you must decide on the path's direction. Consider placing an object on one end and leading the path toward another, final object. In this case, I chose a little house down one path and a patio area at another.

6. Insert an archway into your garden to added effect. This one I made from disposable cocktail forks (made of bamboo). For instructions on how to make these, please see chapter 15.

7. Finally, add a few fairies and see how it transforms the pot of plants into a fairy oasis!

Japonica Garden

I adore Japonicas; they are hardy, have lovely flowers, and attract little birds to your yard. Japonicas are usually easy to work with but I had a poor little sickly plant to work with. However, it keeps going on. Follow these simple instructions and you, too, can create a lovely Japonica garden for your fairies to treasure.

1. I topped the Japonica pot up with desperately needed potting soil.

2. I decided to create this fairy garden with the theme of a washroom. What fairy doesn't need a bathroom, after all?

3. For this theme, you must create an area for the fairy to place her newly washed feet other than dirt. Use colored squares from ceramic coasters bought from a secondhand store to create this effect. Or you may use terracotta tiles from a fairy garden retailer or a craft store.

4. If you have bare soil spots, consider adding additional foliage to the garden. This little creeper with pretty white flowers that bloom in summer does the job nicely.

5.
All you need is a fairy and an accessory and then you are done.

What I adore about this hobby is the ability to change your mind in the blink of an eye. For my Japonica garden, I decided to remove all the items except the newly planted creeper and then added my aquarium bridge.

I then added pebbles at one end of the bridge.

I also replaced the outside toilet and added these sweet little plastic swans, an old candlestick in the front right hand corner, and a fake bonsai to the left on the other side of the bridge.

And a fairy came to admire it all.

But just when everyone thought I'd finished, I changed my mind . . . again.

Out came the bridge and the swans, and they were replaced with the terracotta tile, the matching candlestick holder, and two champagne wire chairs.

Finally, my garden was complete!

Garden in a Basket

This is a lovely activity for a little girl or boy to do all by themselves on a sunny afternoon.

1. Take a basket with a nice long handle and place pebbles in the bottom until covered.

2. Add one artificial bonsai.

3. Then, add a bath tub and a cozy bird's nest for a bed.

4. If there is room, add a champagne wire chair next to the bathtub.

5. Insert a fairy and then she can enjoy her luxury bedroom with its own ensuite.

If you'd rather not make this into a bathroom/bedroom, you can remove the tub and just add a little side table or simply keep the chair and bed.

Another Garden in a Basket

This is another fairy garden that started off as someone else's project. It was given to me as a violet in an old fashioned, slightly falling apart basket. I turned it into a tiny fairy hideaway. If you have any baskets with flowers that need a bit of sprucing up, try adding fairy accessories and resin fairies and see the basket transform.

For this revamped project, I first inserted a bathtub. But it didn't look quite right with the violets.

I thought I'd change the scale of the whole thing and inserted in two little resin houses one each side of the violet.

As these houses were neighbors it was only neighborly to make a path for the fairies to follow to each other's house. And thus, a simple flower basket can be transformed (with little time and effort) into a lovely miniature garden.

Chapter 15

Fairy Furniture and Accessories

There are many online fairy garden accessory retailers and you can also find many of these items in local garden centers and craft stores. While you can buy the loveliest of miniatures for your fairy garden, there is always something very satisfying about making your own. This chapter will give step-by-step instructions on how to construct a variety of fairy-sized garden accessories that won't break the bank. And they are great projects for a rainy day.

Champagne Wire Chair

I confess. I love champagne. I've also always been intrigued by the wire construction that holds the cork into place. The cork itself is a useful thing to have around and I never, ever throw these away—just in case they might come in handy for a fairy garden. Delicate chairs made out of champagne wire are just the thing for fairy gardens. Mine have backs of dried lichen sewn with colored beads to give them an ethereal look, but a plain wire chair also adds a bit of magic to any miniature garden.

For this project you will need:

- 1 champagne wire
- a pair of fine-nosed pliers
- some lichen

- colored beads

- needle

- thread (any color and width)

1. Untwist the wire that runs around what will become the legs of the chair.

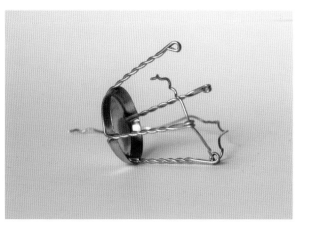

2. When the wire is straight enough pull it out. This is tricky—try not to bend the legs out of shape too much while straightening. One problem is that the metal plate—what will be the seat of the chair—often falls out if the legs are bent too much. If this happens, place it back in and bend the chair legs to hold it into place again. It will now look like a stool.

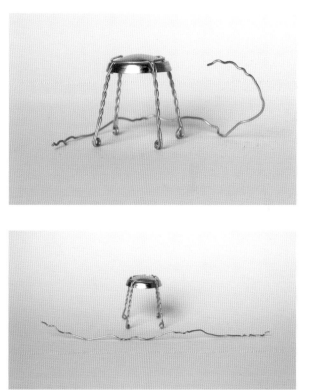

3. With the discarded wire, fashion a back for the chair. Straighten the wire as much as possible.

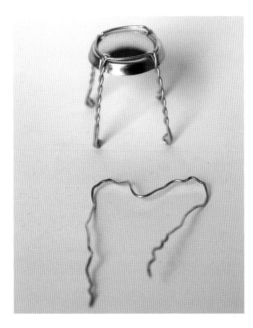

Don't squeeze and bend it too much because it will break. Bend the wire roughly in half. Shape the back of the chair. Make it simple if you are going to cover it with lichen and beads, but if you want just a wire chair, then you will need to use the pliers very carefully and patiently to make a detailed back.

4. Attach the wire back to the stool. Twist one bit of wire onto what will become one of the back legs of the chair and then repeat with the other end of the wire.

You will need to use the pliers to bend the last bit of wire into shape.

5. Now comes the fun part. Thread a needle and use small stitches to secure the lichen to the wire frame of the back of the chair.

Try to match the thread to the lichen, or use a clear nylon thread that will be almost invisible.

When the lichen is secured sort through the beads and push one onto the needle and thread. Stitch into place, repeating until you have the desired effect. Secure and cut the thread.

Twig Chair

For a larger-sized fairy, a simple wire chair won't be enough. For fairies of the larger frame, try making a rustic twig chair instead.

For this project, you will need the following:

- twigs from outside (I typically use twigs from a cotoneaster). The fresher the twigs the less likely they are to snap while being manipulated.

- a roll of florists' or fine gauge wire

- a wire cutter

- a pair of secateurs or scissors that nobody wants any more (cutting twigs and wire ruins scissors)

1. Cut two long lengths of twig. These will be the back and back legs of the chair.

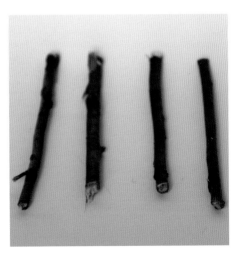

2. Cut two twigs about half the length of the first two. These will be the front legs.

3. Cut four pieces of twig all the same size that will go across the back, each side, and the front. These will form the seat of the chair.

4. Cut another four pieces of twig the same size as those above. These will be used as foot rungs to brace the chair frame.

5. Take the two long back pieces and one of the four cross pieces. Cut a length of wire about five inches long. Holding the cross piece to one of the back pieces, bind them together with the wire. Take the second back piece and hold the cross piece at the same height to it as it is to the one you have just bound.

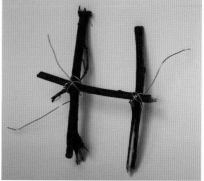

6. Take the two front upright pieces and bind one of the cross pieces to them as you did for the back of the chair

7. Take one of the two remaining cross pieces and join it to the back upright piece and the cross piece, then repeat with the other side.

What you should have is an unmistakable chair shape.

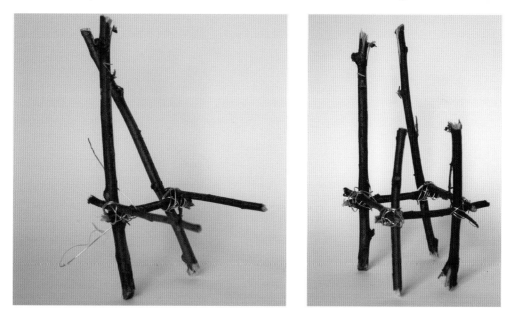

8. You will need to brace the chair with the four remaining cross pieces. These will be placed near the feet of the legs of the chair and are really to help it keep steady but the fairies might want to rest their feet on them, too.

9. The chair will need something for the back rest. For this chair, cut a number of twigs, roughly the same size, that will be wired across the back. Do each rung at a time.

10. The chair is almost complete! For the seat you can wire twigs across as you did for the back. This chair has some plastic netting from a bag that had avocadoes in it. The holes have been placed over the tops of the chair legs and pulled tightly across to form a seat. Make sure to warn your fairies that although this chair is suitable for larger fairies they still can't be very heavy or the chair will collapse.

Four-Poster Bed

A garden can be a luxurious place to take a nap and many fairies will find this delightful rustic bed irresistible.

For assembling this four-poster bed, you will need:

- twigs
- secateurs
- florists' or fine gauge wire
- some lacy fabric for the canopy
- a miniature-sized mattress and pillow

1. This piece of furniture is a variation on the rustic chair only with longer pieces. Cut two long twigs for the back legs and two slightly shorter ones for the front (they can be the same size if you want).

2. Cut two long twigs for the sides of the bed and two short cross pieces to dictate the width of the bed. Take the two back uprights and one cross piece and wire together as you did for the chair.

3. Repeat step 2 for the front legs of the bed.

4. Take the two long pieces and wire them at right angles to the back legs and the cross piece to form the length of the bed.

5. Attach the side pieces to the front of the bed and you will have a rough bed frame.

6. Cut a number of cross pieces to form the base of the bed. Wire these to the two side lengths as you did for the back of the chair.

7. Cut two more side lengths and two more cross pieces to make the canopy frame. This will also help brace the bed. Wire the cross piece to the back legs and front legs and then add the side lengths.

8. Now to make the bed. I used a piece of artificial turf used for model railway displays as the mattress. You could also use lichen or moss, scraps of fabric, or even leaves and flowers. The canopy can be made of torn lace like mine, tulle, crochet, or freshly picked stems of mint.

Ladder

Fairies might have wings but a handmade ladder such as this would be a very attractive thing for them to use in a garden. To make it you will need:

- twigs
- secateurs
- twine or raffia
- scissors

(You can also use florists' wire for a sturdier ladder.)

1. Cut two lengths of sturdy twig. These will be the uprights.

2. Cut a number of short pieces to form the rungs.

3. Cut lengths of twine or raffia and bind one of the cross pieces to one of the uprights. Then bind the other end of the cross piece to the other upright.

4. Continue to do this all the way up the ladder.

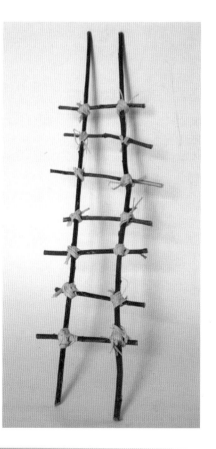

Plastic Four-Poster Fairy Bed or Bower

Recycling is a favorite activity of fairies and they will adore anything you place in a garden that you have repurposed and saved from going into a landfill. The following project is a pretty bed made from an old toy workbench that had been thrown out at the dump. It cost a grand sum of 5 cents. It was faded and unattractive in its original state so something had to be done about it to make it into a lovely garden attraction.

The bench I found had a top and an under-bench, which already looked rather like bunk beds, or, even better, a four-poster bed. I went through all my scraps and selected a tulle type fabric for the side curtains. These were gathered along one side and pulled up and then gathered along the opposite side and pulled up. They were then stitched onto the workbench through the decorative plastic scrolls with a strong thread. Another piece of tulle was lightly gathered for the back of the bed and stitched through the scrolls.

A lace-covered quilted coaster made an ideal covering for the lower bunk and was glued into place. There were two of the coasters, again found at a thrift store, and the matching one was glued onto the top bunk/canopy of the bed with it partly falling over the front. I then pulled apart artificial flowers and rearranged them to form a suitable adornment on each of the top front corners.

The addition of a little glass vase gave the whole bed a rather regal touch and was glued in with a hard-setting glue.

Peg and Cardboard Bed

This is a really simple bed to make for your fairy garden. You will need:

- stiff piece of cardboard
- a handful of half pegs from a craft store
- fast-setting clear glue

1. Cut a rectangle out of the stiff piece of cardboard. The piece I used was from a cardboard box.

2. To make the two bed ends, first place four pegs in a row so they will match the width of the piece of cardboard. Glue one peg across the other four.

3. Place one bed end on the table face up. Glue along one end of the cardboard and place at right angles to the bed end and up against the peg lying across

the others. Have another peg ready, glue, and place it on the other side of the cardboard to help hold it firmly. Hold while it sets.

4. When dry, place the other bed end on the table face up and repeat the process.

5. Paint or decorate bed as you wish to match your garden theme.

Cocktail Fork Arch

An archway can be a delightful addition to any miniature garden and the perfect focal point of the garden or even a nice add-on with a fairy placed beneath it.

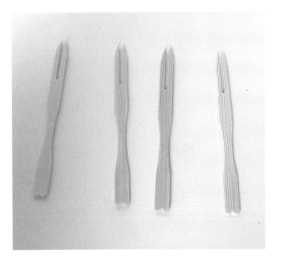

For this craft you will need:

- a packet of bamboo throw away cocktail forks (these are amazing and slot together as if that's what they were designed for)

- 2 mini Popsicle sticks

1. Take four fork—these will be used for the upright panels.

2. Take two additional forks to go along each side of the uprights. Glue together with a fast-drying acrylic glue.

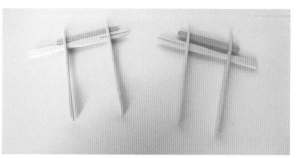

3. Glue the two side pieces together with the mini Popsicle sticks.

Mini Popsicle Stick Picket Fence and Gate

These are miniature versions of the old Popsicle sticks we used to save after having devoured frozen treats. Now, you can buy packets of them at craft stores. For this craft you will need:

- a packet of Popsicle sticks
- two longer Popsicle sticks
- heavy-duty glue

1. Lay your Popsicle sticks in a row on your work surface.

2. Spread glue along the long narrow stick and place it down across the other sticks toward the bottom.

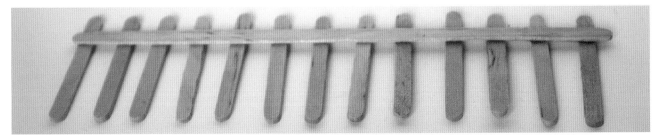

3. Repeat the process with the other long Popsicle stick but place it across the pickets toward the top.

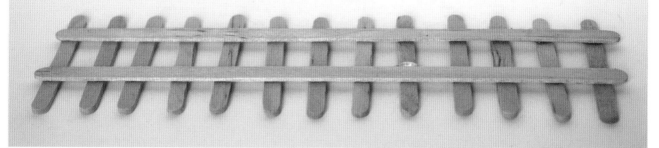

4. And there you have it! An instant fence!

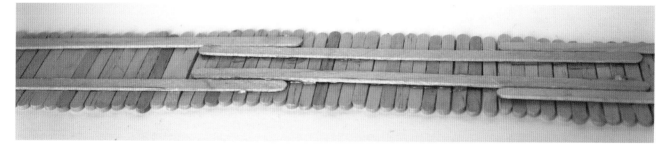

To make the gate:

1. Place the mini Popsicle sticks side by side with no gaps between them.

2. Take another of the sticks and spread with glue. Place onto the five sticks in a diagonal fashion.

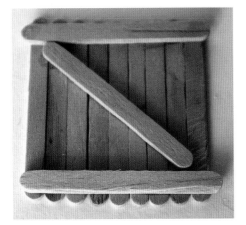

3. Use as a gate or make several and use as mini fences.

Chapter **16**

Homemade Fairies

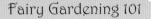

A s mentioned at the beginning of this book, there are plenty of resin or premade fairies that you can purchase from special fairy gardening retailers, garden centers, or craft stores, but if you are on a budget or if you want to make your garden truly unique, here are a few ideas of how to make your own fairies for your garden (and your home!).

Knitted Fairy

Are gardening and knitting exclusive activities? Not at all. What could be better than working hard in the garden all morning and then coming inside and sitting down to an afternoon of knitting in an easy chair? Especially when you are knitting these cute little fairies to play in your garden.

Please note that this fairy is not designed as a toy for children under three years of age.

You will need the following in order to create your own knitted fairy:

- 1 pair 2.25mm needles
- 5 ply yarn in a flesh color
- wool needle
- polyester fiberfil

- mohair, yarn, or embroidery floss for hair
- embroidery thread for features
- 1 toothpick
- 1 pair of artificial butterfly wings

To create the body and head in one piece:

- Cast on 10 stitches.
- Rows 1 to 10: stocking stitch (SS).
- Row 11: k2tog along row (k2tog row) (5).
- Rows 12 to 16: SS 5 rows.
- Row 17: inc. each stitch (knit into front and back of each stitch) (10).
- Row 18: purl (p).
- Row 19: inc. each stitch (20).
- Rows 20 to 28: SS 9 rows.
- Row 29: k2tog row (10).
- Row 30: p.
- Row 31: k2tog row (5).
- Row 32: p and cast off as you go.

To make two legs:

- Cast on 2.
- Row 1: inc. each stitch (4).
- Rows 2 to 26: SS 25 rows casting off on last row.
- Repeat for second leg.

To make two arms:

- Cast on 3.
- Rows 1 to 16: SS 16 rows, cast off on last one.
- Repeat for second arm.

To put it all together:

1. Fold body and head piece in half with the right sides together.

2. Back stitch from the top of the head to just on the base of the skull.

3. Stitch from the bottom of the torso up to the start of the neck.

4. Turn right side out.

5. Stuff the head through the neck opening with tiny pieces of polyester fiberfil. Wrap a toothpick with a wisp of fiberfil and insert up through torso and into head.

6. Stitch the back of the neck closed using a mattress stitch.

7. Add more stuffing to the body if needed.

8. Whip stitch the base of the body closed. **Tip:** Don't overstuff your knitting as the stitches will stretch and show the stuffing. Use the tiniest pieces of stuffing at a time.

9. Fold the arms and legs in half with the right sides out.

10. Mattress stitch them up their length.

11. Sew legs to the base of the body and the arms to the sides.

12. Embroider a tiny face. **Tip:** To make it easier, keep the face simple and use beads for eyes and two stitches for the mouth.

13. Add hair. You can thread each strand of hair through the knitted stitches of the head. You can also glue strands of yarn or mohair onto the head, or you can cut lengths of yarn, fold in half, and stitch straight onto the head in a bundle.

Dressing the Fairy and Adding Wings

Find little bits of lace and ribbon and sew directly onto the body in any way you choose.

If the butterfly you've chosen has antennae they are often made from fine wire. Wrap the antennae around the tops of the fairy's arms and shoulders. Otherwise, sew directly on using nylon thread or a thread the same color as the wings or the fairy.

Now your fairy is ready to fly into the garden.

Cloth Fairy

For those of you who prefer sewing to knitting, this little cloth fairy should satisfy your needs. I have included a pattern at the end of the book that you can photocopy and use to make this fairy.

To make your fairy, collect the following materials:

- calico
- polyester fiberfil
- a fine paintbrush for stuffing
- needle and thread
- fine pencils
- yarn for hair

- bits and pieces for dressing your fairy
- a small pair of artificial butterfly wings

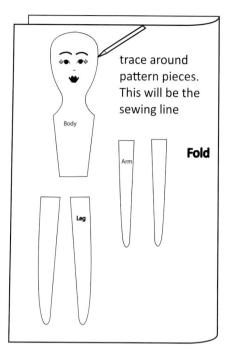

trace around pattern pieces. This will be the sewing line

1. After copying the pattern from page 196, cut out the various pieces.

2. Place the pieces of the pattern on a double layer of calico, and then trace around with a 2b pencil.

3. Sew the pattern before cutting out as it is easier to sew small items this way. All of the pieces here are designed to be sewn first, then cut out of the fabric.

4. Now cut out the sewn pieces and turn right-side out.

5. Take a slim paintbrush, with bristles attached to help hold the stuffing in place, stuff the legs, arms, and body/head. Make sure the body and head are stuffed firmly but the arms and legs can be softer. Stitch all openings shut with a whip stitch.

6. For drawing on the face, use the pencil and draw on the features lightly. Go over with fine pen or embroider the features on.

7. Hair can be stitched or glued, but make sure it's abundant.

8. Now it's time for the fairy's clothes. Remember that the clothes don't need to be removable unless you want them to be. Gather lengths of lace or strips of unhemmed silk, and stitch directly onto the fairy's bodice. Fairies can be quite raggedy like flowers that are starting to fade. I suggest making a skirt first then winding ribbon or lace around the torso for a bodice.

9. Finishing touches to your fairy can include hats, parasols (use those paper umbrellas they put in cocktails), and don't forget to take the butterfly wings and use the wires to attach them to the doll.

Now it's time to try your fairy out in the garden!

Bead Head Fairy

Bead head fairies are quirky little dolls that make excellent visitors to your fairy garden. To make a bead head fairy, you will need:

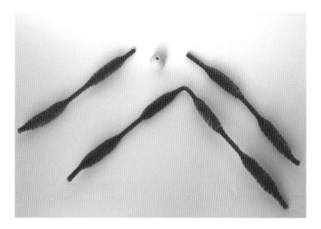

- some wooden beads (not too small and preferably without a varnish on them)
- 2 colored chenille sticks
- fine line pens
- quick-drying acrylic glue
- some fabric flowers of your choosing
- fine lace or ribbon for the bodice
- a pair of artificial butterfly wings

1 Choose one stick for the legs, bend in half, and insert bent end into the bead, leaving approximately 1 cm protruding. Then bend this over.

2. Twist the stick a couple of times under the bead to form a neck.

3. Take another stick and bend slightly in the middle. Insert it between the upright sticks.

4. Twist the upright sticks together to form the torso and the two legs.

5. Bend the feet over a little and the hands so that the wire doesn't poke into your fingers.

6. Fairies quite often like to be dressed in their favorite flower petals. I do believe that rose petals are back in this season, so make sure you have some among your fake flowers. Pull the petals off the stem and separate them.

7. Choose three or four petals that you like in combination—they don't all need to be from one type of flower; they just need to look good together.

8. Push the petals up the legs of the fairy in the order you want them. When you have them the way you want, turn the fairy upside down and put a dab of glue to keep the petals in place.

9. Take a piece of ribbon and wrap it around the arms and torso. Then glue or stitch into place.

10. Choose the finest of your fine-tipped pens and make a face for your fairy. It can be simple dots for eyes and nothing more, although I prefer my fairies to also have a heart-shaped mouth. Noses can be a problem to make, so simply draw a small slash over the mouth or two dots (or if you feel skilful then draw a fine nose down the center of her face).

11. To complete your fairy, you will need to add hair or perhaps a hat. If the hat is big and floppy you won't need hair. Otherwise use curly nylon doll hair from the craft store, a bit of unspun wool, or fine embroidery thread. Glue the hair pieces to the head, making sure the hair doesn't cover up the fairy's face.

12. If you'd like to add a hat to your fairy, which will make her look dressed for a nice walk in the garden, find some smaller petals from among the dismembered artificial flowers. Unbend the chenille stick if it isn't too buried under the hair, slip the petal onto the stick, and bend it back over. Otherwise, glue the petal hat in place atop the hair.

13.
All that's left to do now is attach some wings. I prefer buying beautiful butterflies from the craft store to use as wings. Use the fine wire on the butterflies to twist under the fairy's arms and around the torso to keep them in place. Now your fairy is ready to visit the garden.

Chapter 17

Fairy Garden Gallery

Making fairy gardens has been so much fun that I decided to ask friends and colleagues to join me in creating their own magical miniature gardens. Here is a selection of their best efforts and the beautiful (and creative!) fairy gardens they made. I hope you will find inspiration in these gardens for your very own magical miniature world!

Charlotte's Fairy Paradise

Charlotte is four years old and is an expert in fairy gardens. With the help of her mom, Jo-Ann, she has created a wonderfully fun and diverse environment to attract fairies to play in.

Jo-Ann insists that Charlotte was the designer and a very demanding one, too. Jo-Ann was nothing more than a helper in this garden's creation.

Sophie's Queen of Hearts Garden

Sophie Masson is the author of *Moonlight and Ashes, Scarlet in the Snow, The Boggle Hunters, Two Trickster Tales from Russia,* and many other books for children and young adults. When I asked her if she would like to contribute a fairy garden to my gallery, she didn't hesitate.

Sophie's garden is completely different to what many would think of as a garden but you can see the writer's intellect breaking through with the *Alice in Wonderland* references. Sophie has this to say about this particular garden:

The Queen of Hearts Garden is inspired by the character of the fairy of that name, who appears in the ever-popular *Alice in Wonderland*. The Queen of Hearts is not a sweet, kind fairy; she's harsh and dictatorial and, being a dream-type character, has absurd rules. But she also loves order and symmetry. In her world, paths must follow straight lines and flowers must be in neat rows and in the right colors—she's ready to chop off her gardeners' heads if they plant the wrong color rose. And so they've been busy with pots of paint to turn white roses into red—but she has just glided into her garden in her winged car and caught them at it!

She doesn't like anyone else coming into her garden and so has caged it and put warning signs on it. You can see through the bars and the cage can easily be lifted off, showing how little she does control, despite her efforts. After all, Alice can just tell her, "You're nothing but a pack of cards!" The Queen of Hearts' world is topsy-turvy—hence the mirrored ground, which reflects the world upside down. The mirror's also a hint towards the second book, *Through the Looking-Glass*.

Patti Kuhlman's Gardens

Patti Kuhlman of Wholesale Fairy Gardens has this to say about her creative process:

Fairy Gardening is an activity that allows your mind to escape the time zone you are in and to relive your childhood memories. Many different pictures can be created when you are building your own fairy garden. They are relaxing to look at: the serenity takes over, causing you to wish you yourself were in the fairy houses. Creativity is built by imagination. I like to look at the pieces in front of me, close my eyes, and visualize. I visualize where I could see the scene I am about to create. Once my imagination is on board, I just start building. I have never built two fairy gardens that look the same, and that's the beauty of creativity. Everything and everyone is unique.

Planting has always been an outdoor activity that I enjoyed. After discovering fairy gardens, and combining them, it was an overwhelming feeling seeing your live plants and your Fairy items creating such beautiful images.

Jessie's Tonkadale Greenhouse Gardens

These beautiful gardens come courtesy of Jessie Jacobson and Tonkadale Greenhouse.

Ronna Moore's Fairy Homes and Gardens

Ronna Moore is the artistic director behind Fairy Homes and Gardens.

Roberta's Market Hill Gardens

Roberta Smith of Market Hill created these delightful gardens oases.

Acknowledgments

First, I would like to thank Julie Matysik of Skyhorse Publishing, editor extraordinaire. Second, I thank my lovely, patient literary agent, Isabel Atherton of Creative Authors. These two women look after me as if I were writing royalty.

Thank you also to all the people who contributed gardens to this book: Roberta Smith, Jessie Jacobson, Patti Kuhlman, Ronna Moore, Sophie Masson, Charlotte and Jo-Ann Fletcher, and Peta Ryan.

I'd like to thank my daughter Beattie Alvarez for her photography and editing help and my wonderful mother who put up with months of fairy garden stuff cluttering the living room.

As always, a big thanks to the backroom boys and girls who put words and pictures into book form and make them come to life.

Pattern for the Cloth Fairy found on page 177.

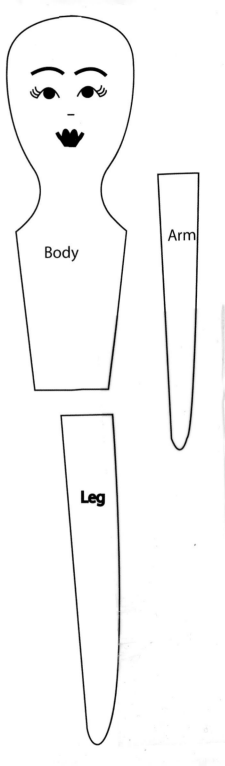